A.Wainwright

A WALKER'S
NOTEBOOK

F

FRANCES LINCOLN LIMITED
PUBLISHERS

Frances Lincoln Limited
4 Torriano Mews
Torriano Avenue
London NW5 2RZ
www.franceslincoln.com

British Library cataloguing-in-publication data
A catalogue record for this book is available
from the British Library

ISBN: 978-0-7112-2823-8

Printed in China
First Frances Lincoln edition 2007
Reprinted 2008

The fleeting hour of life of those who love the hills is quickly spent, but the hills are eternal. Always there will be the lonely ridge, the dancing beck, the silent forest; always there will be the exhilaration of the summits. These are for the seeking, and those who seek and find while there is yet time will be blessed both in mind and body.

I wish you all many happy days on the fells in the years ahead.

AWainwright

Looking backwards
(between one's legs)
there is a superb
upside-down view
of Wasdale Head

Finder, please return to

IN CASE OF EMERGENCY PLEASE CONTACT:

EMERGENCY CONTACT NUMBERS

For mountain rescue and coastguard help dial 999 or 112

OTHER USEFUL NUMBERS

WEATHER INFORMATION

www.weathercall.co.uk

Weathercall offers a 10-day Met Office weather forecast. The forecast begins with a 24-hour regional summary followed by a 5-day weather forecast for the local area selected. A national summary follows for days 6-10 and then the month ahead.

(Calls cost 60p per minute from a UK landline. Calls from mobiles may be subject to network operator surcharges)

Weathercall areas	Telephone no.
National UK	09068 500 400
Greater London	09068 500 401
Kent, Surrey & Sussex	09068 500 402
Dorset, Hampshire & Isle of Wight	09068 500 403
Devon & Cornwall	09068 500 404
Wiltshire, Gloucestershire, Avon & Somerset	09068 500 405
Berkshire, Buckinghamshire & Oxon	09068 500 406
Bedfordshire, Hertfordshire & Essex	09068 500 407
Norfolk, Suffolk & Cambridgeshire	09068 500 408
South Wales	09068 500 409
Shropshire, Herefordshire & Worcestershire	09068 500 410
West Midlands, Staffordshire & Warwicks	09068 500 411
Notts, Leics, Northants & Derbyshire	09068 500 412

[Note: The Publisher cannot accept responsibility for the content of any external websites.]

Lincolnshire	09068 500 413
Mid Wales	09068 500 414
North Wales	09068 500 415
North West of England	09068 500 416
East Riding, York & S/W/N Yorkshire	09068 500 417
Durham, Northumberland, Tyne & Wear	09068 500 418
Cumbria, Lake District & Isle of Man	09068 500 419
Dumfries & Galloway	09068 500 420
Central Scotland & Strathclyde	09068 500 421
Fife, Lothian & Borders	09068 500 422
Tayside	09068 500 423
Grampian & East Highlands	09068 500 424
West Highlands & Islands	09068 500 425
Caithness, Sutherland, Orkney & Shetland Is	09068 500 426
Northern Ireland	09068 500 427

Local Weather Forecast via SMS

Receive the latest local weather forecast as a text message to your mobile (charge per message applies).

To receive your 5-day forecast: Create a text message, type WC 5DAY plus the name of the LOCATION and send to 83141

"Please can you tell me where the Pennine Way is?"

TRAFFIC & TRAVEL INFORMATION

The latest on road traffic and travel conditions is available from the following services. All calls are subject to a charge.

Road

Landline:	09068 020 541 (RAC)
	09003 401 100 (AA)
Mobile:	Call 1740 (RAC Live)
	Call 401 100 (AA Roadwatch)
	O2 Customers: Call Trafficline on 1200
	Vodafone customers: Call 2222
	T-Mobile customers: Call 2020
	Orange customers: Call 117

Rail

Network Rail for timetables www.networkrail.co.uk
National Rail Enquiries for reservations www.nationalrail.co.uk

Bus

National Express for coach travel www.nationalexpress.com
UK Bus Timetable website directory
http://timetables.showbus.co.uk

General travel

Travel Planning portal
www.traveline.org.uk

Admittedly,
these illustrations
have nothing to do
with the Outlying Fells.
Makes a nice change from
drawing mountains, though.

USEFUL ORGANIZATIONS & WEBSITES

The following websites contain information on walking, destinations and equipment.

The Ramblers Association (Britain's biggest walking charity) www.ramblers.org.uk

The Woodland Trust (access details to over 1,000 woods) www.woodland-trust.org.uk

The National Trust www.nationaltrust.org.uk

The National Trust for Scotland www.nts.org.uk

National Trails (information on 2,500 miles of trails in England, Wales & Scotland) www.nationaltrail.co.uk

The Ordnance Survey (buy or download maps online) www.ordnancesurvey.co.uk

Harvey Maps (for walking, hiking, rambling and cycling maps) www.harveymaps.co.uk

Walking in Britain www.walkingbritain.co.uk

Walking in Scotland www.walkscotland.com

Lake District National Park Authority www.lake-district.gov.uk

Cumbria Tourist Board site www.golakes.co.uk

Yorkshire Tourist Board site www.yorkshire.com

South West of England Tourist Board site www.swtourism.co.uk

South East England Tourist Board site www.visitsoutheastengland.com

North East England Tourist Board site www.visitnortheastengland.com

Scottish Tourist Board site www.visitscotland.com

Welsh Tourist Board site www.visitwales.com

Ireland's Tourist Board site www.ireland.ie

NAISMITH'S RULE

Naismith's rule allows an easy calculation of the time taken for a hill walk, for a reasonably fit and steady walker. The rule was devised in 1892 by W. W. Naismith, a Scottish mountaineer.

The rule states that a fit person will travel at an average of 5 kilometres per hour, and will take an extra 30 minutes for every 300 metres of ascent.

For ascents you need to remember to take into account every metre climbed. For example if you ascend 100 metres, descend for 50 metres, and then ascend again for a further 150 metres, although you have only gained 200 metres of height, you have actually climbed 250 metres, and it is this full amount that must be taken into consideration.

Also consider that in poor visibility and rough terrain you will almost certainly move more slowly than the rule suggests, perhaps at 3 or 4km per hour. You will also travel more slowly at the end of the day.

Naismith's Rule should only be used as a rough guide and your estimate should take into account the prevailing conditions and should always be calculated for the slowest person in the walking group.

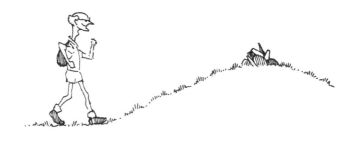

BEFORE YOU LEAVE – A CHECKLIST

- Water
- Food
- Plastic bag to carry your rubbish away
- Warm clothing
- First Aid kit including blister care
- Map
- Compass and navigation equipment
- Hat
- Gloves
- Sun protection cream
- Camera
- Torch
- Mobile phone (Mobile phone coverage in hilly areas can be very limited. You can check coverage before you go at: www.gsmworld.com)

Finally, have you left details with a third party of where you are going and when you are expecting to be back?

START LOCATION   Kinross

DATE(S) WALKED   6/2 2010

START TIME: 10.30   FINISH TIME: 2.30

ROUTE/ASCENT(S)/DESCENT(S) USED

Dougs walk / Rem Gless.

COMMENTS (walking companions, weather, observations, experiences etc)

16

START LOCATION _Carl Pen Pub._

DATE(S) WALKED _14/2/2010_

START TIME: _10.45 am_ FINISH TIME: _2.00pm_

ROUTE/ASCENT(S)/DESCENT(S) USED
Ascent   Lucklaw Hill

COMMENTS (walking companions, weather, observations, experiences etc)

TAKE CARE
DO NOT
START
FIRE

and so waste the effort
spent in drawing all the
little trees on this map.
The Forestry Commission,
too, will be annoyed.

17

START LOCATION ....

DATE(S) WALKED ....

START TIME: .... FINISH TIME: ....

ROUTE/ASCENT(S)/DESCENT(S) USED

....

....

....

....

....

....

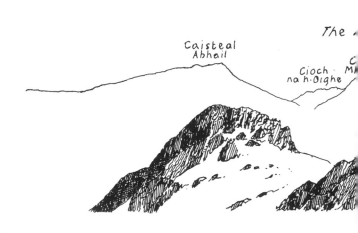

COMMENTS (walking companions, weather, observations, experiences etc)

....

....

....

....

....

....

....

....

....

....

....

in skyline, seen from Beinn Bharrain

START LOCATION ....

DATE(S) WALKED ....

START TIME: .... FINISH TIME: ....

ROUTE/ASCENT(S)/DESCENT(S) USED

....

....

....

COMMENTS (walking companions, weather, observations, experiences etc)

....

....

....

....

....

....

....

....

....

People with bad coughs should keep out of the line of fall

START LOCATION .... ‑ ....

DATE(S) WALKED ....

START TIME: .... FINISH TIME: ....

ROUTE/ASCENT(S)/DESCENT(S) USED

....

....

....

COMMENTS (walking companions, weather, observations, experiences etc)

....

....

....

....

....

....

....

....

....

....

....

The monument
(19th century)
marks the spot
where Henry VI
was found,
by shepherds,
wandering after the
Battle of Towton in
1461. He was taken
to the Castle and
sheltered there.

The monument

START LOCATION ....

DATE(S) WALKED ....

START TIME: .... FINISH TIME: ....

ROUTE/ASCENT(S)/DESCENT(S) USED

....

....

....

COMMENTS (walking companions, weather, observations, experiences etc)

....

....

....

....

....

....

....

....

....

....

....

START LOCATION

DATE(S) WALKED

START TIME: FINISH TIME:

ROUTE/ASCENT(S)/DESCENT(S) USED

COMMENTS (walking companions, weather, observations, experiences etc)

Circular sheepfold.
Wiley Gill

START LOCATION ....

DATE(S) WALKED ....

START TIME: .... FINISH TIME: ....

ROUTE/ASCENT(S)/DESCENT(S) USED

....

....

....

COMMENTS (walking companions, weather, observations, experiences etc)

....

....

....

....

START LOCATION ....

DATE(S) WALKED ....

START TIME: .... FINISH TIME: ....

ROUTE/ASCENT(S)/DESCENT(S) USED

....

....

....

COMMENTS (walking companions, weather, observations, experiences etc)

....

....

....

....

....

....

....

....

....

....

....

....

START LOCATION ....

DATE(S) WALKED ....

START TIME: .... FINISH TIME: ....

ROUTE/ASCENT(S)/DESCENT(S) USED

....

....

....

COMMENTS (walking companions, weather, observations, experiences etc)

....

....

....

....

....

....

....

....

....

....

....

Malham Cove

START LOCATION ....

DATE(S) WALKED ....

START TIME: .... FINISH TIME: ....

ROUTE/ASCENT(S)/DESCENT(S) USED

....

....

....

COMMENTS (walking companions, weather, observations, experiences etc)

....

....

....

....

....

....

....

....

....

....

....

START LOCATION ....

DATE(S) WALKED ....

START TIME: .... FINISH TIME: ....

ROUTE/ASCENT(S)/DESCENT(S) USED

....

....

....

COMMENTS (walking companions, weather, observations, experiences etc)

....

....

....

....

....

....

....

....

....

....

....

....

Rock formations on Green Pikes

START LOCATION ....

DATE(S) WALKED ....

START TIME: .... FINISH TIME: ....

ROUTE/ASCENT(S)/DESCENT(S) USED

....

....

....

COMMENTS (walking companions, weather, observations, experiences etc)

....

....

....

....

Broad Stand

NOT FOR WALKERS

entrance

START LOCATION ....

DATE(S) WALKED ....

START TIME: .... FINISH TIME: ....

ROUTE/ASCENT(S)/DESCENT(S) USED

....

....

....

COMMENTS (walking companions, weather, observations, experiences etc)

....

....

....

....

....

....

....

....

....

....

.... 200 ....

HE'LL NEVER
DO IT!

START LOCATION ....

DATE(S) WALKED ....

START TIME: .... FINISH TIME: ....

ROUTE/ASCENT(S)/DESCENT(S) USED

....

....

....

COMMENTS (walking companions, weather, observations, experiences etc)

....

....

....

....

....

....

....

....

....

....

....

....

....

START LOCATION

DATE(S) WALKED

START TIME: FINISH TIME:

ROUTE/ASCENT(S)/DESCENT(S) USED

COMMENTS (walking companions, weather, observations, experiences etc)

A negative signpost
(intended to help motorists)
Kirkstile Inn road junction

START LOCATION ....

DATE(S) WALKED ....

START TIME: .... FINISH TIME: ....

ROUTE/ASCENT(S)/DESCENT(S) USED

....

....

....

COMMENTS (walking companions, weather, observations, experiences etc)

....

....

....

....

....

....

....

....

....

....

....

....

START LOCATION ....

DATE(S) WALKED ....

START TIME: .... FINISH TIME: ....

ROUTE/ASCENT(S)/DESCENT(S) USED

....

....

....

COMMENTS (walking companions, weather, observations, experiences etc)

....

....

....

....

....

....

....

....

....

....

.... 300 ....

....

START LOCATION ....

DATE(S) WALKED ....

START TIME: ....   FINISH TIME: ....

ROUTE/ASCENT(S)/DESCENT(S) USED

....

....

....

Limestone pinnacle.
Penyghent

COMMENTS

....

....

....

....

....

....

....

....

....

....

....

....

START LOCATION ....

DATE(S) WALKED ....

START TIME: .... FINISH TIME: ....

ROUTE/ASCENT(S)/DESCENT(S) USED

....

....

....

COMMENTS (walking companions, weather, observations, experiences etc)

....

....

....

....

....

....

....

....

....

....

....

....

Ullswater
from the
north-east ridge

START LOCATION ....

DATE(S) WALKED ....

START TIME: .... FINISH TIME: ....

ROUTE/ASCENT(S)/DESCENT(S) USED

....

....

....

COMMENTS (walking companions, weather, observations, experiences etc)

....

....

....

....

....

....

....

*Brae Fell
from the Caldbeck road
near Fell Side*

START LOCATION ....

DATE(S) WALKED ....

START TIME: .... FINISH TIME: ....

ROUTE/ASCENT(S)/DESCENT(S) USED

....

....

....

COMMENTS (walking companions, weather, observations, experiences etc)

....

....

....

....

....

....

....

....

....

....

....

....

START LOCATION ....

DATE(S) WALKED ....

START TIME: .... FINISH TIME: ....

ROUTE/ASCENT(S)/DESCENT(S) USED

....

....

....

COMMENTS (walking companions, weather, observations, experiences etc)

....

....

....

....

....

Moss Eccles Tarn

START LOCATION ....

DATE(S) WALKED ....

START TIME: .... FINISH TIME: ....

ROUTE/ASCENT(S)/DESCENT(S) USED

....

....

....

COMMENTS (walking companions, weather, observations, experiences etc)

....

....

....

....

....

....

Wise Een Tarn

START LOCATION ....

DATE(S) WALKED ....

START TIME: .... FINISH TIME: ....

ROUTE/ASCENT(S)/DESCENT(S) USED

....

....

....

COMMENTS (walking companions, weather, observations, experiences etc)

....

....

....

....

....

....

....

....

....

....

....

....

....

The Pudding Stone
(the easy side)

*It is perhaps
unnecessary
to add that the
figure up aloft
is not the author*

START LOCATION ....

DATE(S) WALKED ....

START TIME: .... FINISH TIME: ....

ROUTE/ASCENT(S)/DESCENT(S) USED

....

....

....

COMMENTS (walking companions, weather, observations, experiences etc)

....

....

....

....

....

....

....

....

....

....

....

....

START LOCATION

DATE(S) WALKED

START TIME: .... FINISH TIME: ....

ROUTE/ASCENT(S)/DESCENT(S) USED

COMMENTS (walking companions, weather, observations, experiences etc)

Swindale
with Selside Pike at the head of the valley

START LOCATION ....

DATE(S) WALKED ....

START TIME: .... FINISH TIME: ....

ROUTE/ASCENT(S)/DESCENT(S) USED

....

....

....

COMMENTS (walking companions, weather, observations, experiences etc)

....

....

....

....

....

Swindale Head

START LOCATION ....

DATE(S) WALKED ....

START TIME: .... FINISH TIME: ....

ROUTE/ASCENT(S)/DESCENT(S) USED

....

....

....

COMMENTS (walking companions, weather, observations, experiences etc)

....

....

....

....

....

....

....

....

....

Path in the heather.
Caldew Valley
at the base of Knott
(Carrock Fell in the background)

START LOCATION ....

DATE(S) WALKED ....

START TIME: .... FINISH TIME: ....

ROUTE/ASCENT(S)/DESCENT(S) USED

....

....

....

COMMENTS (walking companions, weather, observations, experiences etc)

....

....

....

....

....

....

....

....

....

....

....

....

....

START LOCATION ....

DATE(S) WALKED ....

START TIME: .... FINISH TIME: ....

ROUTE/ASCENT(S)/DESCENT(S) USED

....

....

....

COMMENTS (walking companions, weather, observations, experiences etc)

....

....

....

....

....

....

....

....

....

....

....

from Catherstone Head

51

START LOCATION ....

DATE(S) WALKED ....

START TIME: .... FINISH TIME: ....

ROUTE/ASCENT(S)/DESCENT(S) USED

....

....

....

COMMENTS (walking companions, weather, observations, experiences etc)

....

....

....

....

....

Gray Bull

Persons over 75 years of age
are advised to regard it
as unclimbable

START LOCATION ....

DATE(S) WALKED ....

START TIME: .... FINISH TIME: ....

ROUTE/ASCENT(S)/DESCENT(S) USED

....

....

....

COMMENTS (walking companions, weather, observations, experiences etc)

....

....

....

....

....

....

....

....

....

....

....

START LOCATION ....

DATE(S) WALKED ....

START TIME: .... FINISH TIME: ....

ROUTE/ASCENT(S)/DESCENT(S) USED

....

....

....

COMMENTS (walking companions, weather, observations, experiences etc)

....

....

....

....

....

....

....

....

....

....

....

....

START LOCATION ....

DATE(S) WALKED ....

START TIME: .... FINISH TIME: ....

ROUTE/ASCENT(S)/DESCENT(S) USED

....

....

....

COMMENTS (walking companions, weather, observations, experiences etc)

....

....

....

....

....

....

....

....

....

....

....

....

START LOCATION ....

DATE(S) WALKED ....

START TIME: .... FINISH TIME: ....

ROUTE/ASCENT(S)/DESCENT(S) USED

....

....

....

COMMENTS (walking companions, weather, observations, experiences etc)

....

....

....

....

....

....

RED PIKE   SCOAT FELL   PILLAR   CRAG FELL

looking west

START LOCATION ....

DATE(S) WALKED ....

START TIME: .... FINISH TIME: ....

ROUTE/ASCENT(S)/DESCENT(S) USED

....

....

....

COMMENTS (walking companions, weather, observations, experiences etc)

....

....

....

....

....

....

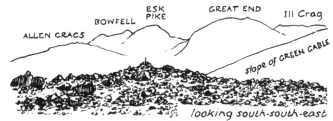

START LOCATION ....

DATE(S) WALKED ....

START TIME: .... FINISH TIME: ....

ROUTE/ASCENT(S)/DESCENT(S) USED

....

....

....

COMMENTS (walking companions, weather, observations, experiences etc)

....

....

....

looking south-south-east
from Lanthwaite Hill

START LOCATION ....

DATE(S) WALKED ....

START TIME: .... FINISH TIME: ....

ROUTE/ASCENT(S)/DESCENT(S) USED

....

....

....

COMMENTS (walking companions, weather, observations, experiences etc)

....

....

....

....

....

....

....

....

....

....

....

....

START LOCATION ....

DATE(S) WALKED ....

START TIME: .... FINISH TIME: ....

ROUTE/ASCENT(S)/DESCENT(S) USED

....

....

....

COMMENTS (walking companions, weather, observations, experiences etc)

....

....

....

....

....

....

....

....

....

....

....

START LOCATION ....

DATE(S) WALKED ....

START TIME: .... FINISH TIME: ....

ROUTE/ASCENT(S)/DESCENT(S) USED

....

....

....

COMMENTS (walking companions, weather, observations, experiences etc)

....

....

....

....

....

....

....

....

....

....

....

....

START LOCATION ....

DATE(S) WALKED ....

START TIME: .... FINISH TIME: ....

ROUTE/ASCENT(S)/DESCENT(S) USED

....

....

....

COMMENTS (walking companions, weather, observations, experiences etc)

....

....

....

....

....

....

....

....

....

....

....

....

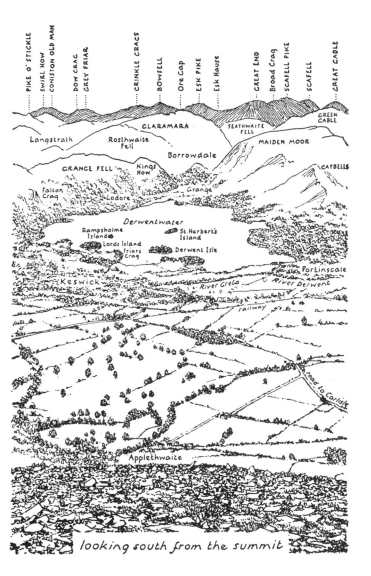

looking south from the summit

START LOCATION ....

DATE(S) WALKED ....

START TIME: .... FINISH TIME: ....

ROUTE/ASCENT(S)/DESCENT(S) USED

....

....

....

COMMENTS (walking companions, weather, observations, experiences etc)

....

....

....

....

....

....

....

START LOCATION ....

DATE(S) WALKED ....

START TIME: .... FINISH TIME: ....

ROUTE/ASCENT(S)/DESCENT(S) USED

....

....

....

COMMENTS (walking companions, weather, observations, experiences etc)

....

....

....

....

....

....

....

....

....

....

....

START LOCATION

DATE(S) WALKED

START TIME: FINISH TIME:

ROUTE/ASCENT(S)/DESCENT(S) USED

COMMENTS (walking companions, weather, observations, experiences etc)

from Mungrisdale,
obviously

(Telegraph poles removed from this view without permission of the P.O. Engineers)

START LOCATION ....

DATE(S) WALKED ....

START TIME: .... FINISH TIME: ....

ROUTE/ASCENT(S)/DESCENT(S) USED

....

....

....

COMMENTS (walking companions, weather, observations, experiences etc)

....

....

....

....

....

....

....

....

....

....

....

....

START LOCATION ....

DATE(S) WALKED ....

START TIME: .... FINISH TIME: ....

ROUTE/ASCENT(S)/DESCENT(S) USED

....

....

....

COMMENTS (walking companions, weather, observations, experiences etc)

....

....

....

....

....

On the top of
Binsey..........

...... Prehistoric
Tumulus
and
Ancient
Briton

START LOCATION ....

DATE(S) WALKED ....

START TIME: .... FINISH TIME: ....

ROUTE/ASCENT(S)/DESCENT(S) USED

....

....

....

COMMENTS (walking companions, weather, observations, experiences etc)

....

....

....

....

....

....

....

....

....

....

....

....

START LOCATION ....

DATE(S) WALKED ....

START TIME: .... FINISH TIME: ....

ROUTE/ASCENT(S)/DESCENT(S) USED

....

....

....

COMMENTS (walking companions, weather, observations, experiences etc)

....

....

....

....

....

....

....

....

....

....

....

START LOCATION ....

DATE(S) WALKED ....

START TIME: .... FINISH TIME: ....

ROUTE/ASCENT(S)/DESCENT(S) USED

....

....

....

COMMENTS (walking companions, weather, observations, experiences etc)

....

....

....

....

....

....

....

High Sweden Bridge

START LOCATION ....

DATE(S) WALKED ....

START TIME: .... FINISH TIME: ....

ROUTE/ASCENT(S)/DESCENT(S) USED

....

....

....

COMMENTS (walking companions, weather, observations, experiences etc)

....

....

....

....

....

....

Grasmere
from Loughrigg Terrace

START LOCATION ....

DATE(S) WALKED ....

START TIME: .... FINISH TIME: ....

ROUTE/ASCENT(S)/DESCENT(S) USED

....

....

....

COMMENTS (walking companions, weather, observations, experiences etc)

....

....

....

....

....

....

....

....

....

....

....

START LOCATION

DATE(S) WALKED

START TIME: FINISH TIME:

ROUTE/ASCENT(S)/DESCENT(S) USED

COMMENTS (walking companions, weather, observations, experiences etc)

Haweswater
from the third cairn

START LOCATION ....

DATE(S) WALKED ....

START TIME: .... FINISH TIME: ....

ROUTE/ASCENT(S)/DESCENT(S) USED

....

....

....

COMMENTS (walking companions, weather, observations, experiences etc)

....

....

....

....

....

....

....

....

....

....

....

START LOCATION ....

DATE(S) WALKED ....

START TIME: .... FINISH TIME: ....

ROUTE/ASCENT(S)/DESCENT(S) USED

....

....

....

COMMENTS (walking companions, weather, observations, experiences etc)

....

....

....

....

....

....

THE SUMMIT

Tourists looking for Blackpool Tower

Boy Scouts

Typical summit scene

Solitary fellwalker, bless him, looking north to the hills

START LOCATION ....

DATE(S) WALKED ....

START TIME: .... FINISH TIME: ....

ROUTE/ASCENT(S)/DESCENT(S) USED

....

....

....

COMMENTS (walking companions, weather, observations, experiences etc)

....

....

....

....

....

....

....

....

....

....

....

START LOCATION ....

DATE(S) WALKED ....

START TIME: .... FINISH TIME: ....

ROUTE/ASCENT(S)/DESCENT(S) USED

....

....

....

COMMENTS (walking companions, weather, observations, experiences etc)

....

....

....

....

....

....

....

....

....

....

....

Cloven Stone

START LOCATION

DATE(S) WALKED

START TIME: FINISH TIME:

ROUTE/ASCENT(S)/DESCENT(S) USED

COMMENTS (walking companions, weather, observations, experiences etc)

The summit, from Striding Edge

START LOCATION ....

DATE(S) WALKED ....

START TIME: .... FINISH TIME: ....

ROUTE/ASCENT(S)/DESCENT(S) USED

....

....

....

COMMENTS (walking companions, weather, observations, experiences etc)

....

....

....

....

....

....

....

....

....

....

....

....

START LOCATION ....

DATE(S) WALKED ....

START TIME: .... FINISH TIME: ....

ROUTE/ASCENT(S)/DESCENT(S) USED

....

....

....

COMMENTS (walking companions, weather, observations, experiences etc)

....

....

....

....

....

....

....

....

....

....

....

....

START LOCATION ....

DATE(S) WALKED ....

START TIME: .... FINISH TIME: ....

ROUTE/ASCENT(S)/DESCENT(S) USED

....

....

....

COMMENTS (walking companions, weather, observations, experiences etc)

....

....

....

....

....

....

....

....

....

....

....

....

....

....

Napes Needle

definitely
not the
← author!

START LOCATION ....

DATE(S) WALKED ....

START TIME: .... FINISH TIME: ....

ROUTE/ASCENT(S)/DESCENT(S) USED

....

....

....

COMMENTS (walking companions, weather, observations, experiences etc)

....

....

....

....

....

....

....

....

....

....

START LOCATION ....

DATE(S) WALKED ....

START TIME: .... FINISH TIME: ....

ROUTE/ASCENT(S)/DESCENT(S) USED

....

....

....

COMMENTS (walking companions, weather, observations, experiences etc)

....

....

....

....

....

....

....

....

....

....

....

Red Deer
Stag

START LOCATION ....

DATE(S) WALKED ....

START TIME: .... FINISH TIME: ....

ROUTE/ASCENT(S)/DESCENT(S) USED

....

....

....

COMMENTS (walking companions, weather, observations, experiences etc)

....

....

....

....

....

....

....

....

....

....

....

.... 400 ....

START LOCATION

DATE(S) WALKED

START TIME: FINISH TIME:

ROUTE/ASCENT(S)/DESCENT(S) USED

COMMENTS (walking companions, weather, observations, experiences etc)

*"... a massive heap of stones
calls for investigation...."*

What is its purpose, if any?
It is not a tumulus.
It is not a cairn.
It is not a wall.
It is not a bield.
It is not indicated on Ordnance maps.
It has an air of permanence but not of antiquity.
It could be nothing more than a collection of stones
cleared from the adjacent forest in the course of planting.

START LOCATION ....

DATE(S) WALKED ....

START TIME: .... FINISH TIME: ....

ROUTE/ASCENT(S)/DESCENT(S) USED

....

....

....

COMMENTS (walking companions, weather, observations, experiences etc)

....

....

....

....

....

....

....

....

....

....

....

....

START LOCATION ....

DATE(S) WALKED ....

START TIME: ....   FINISH TIME: ....

ROUTE/ASCENT(S)/DESCENT(S) USED

....

....

....

COMMENTS (walking companions, weather, observations, experiences etc)

....

....

....

....

....

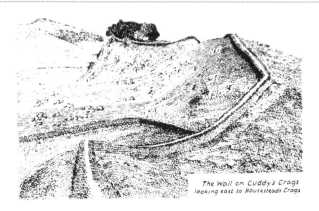

The Wall on Cuddy's Crags
looking east to Housesteads Crags

START LOCATION ....

DATE(S) WALKED ....

START TIME: .... FINISH TIME: ....

ROUTE/ASCENT(S)/DESCENT(S) USED

....

....

....

COMMENTS (walking companions, weather, observations, experiences etc)

....

....

....

....

....

....

....

....

....

....

....

....

START LOCATION ....

DATE(S) WALKED ....

START TIME: .... FINISH TIME: ....

ROUTE/ASCENT(S)/DESCENT(S) USED

....
....
....

COMMENTS (walking companions, weather, observations, experiences etc)

....
....
....
....
....
....
....
....
....
....
....
....

START LOCATION ....

DATE(S) WALKED ....

START TIME: .... FINISH TIME: ....

ROUTE/ASCENT(S)/DESCENT(S) USED

....

....

....

COMMENTS (walking companions, weather, observations, experiences etc)

....

....

....

....

....

....

Derelict cottage and air shaft,
    Lambley Colliery

START LOCATION ....

DATE(S) WALKED ....

START TIME: .... FINISH TIME: ....

ROUTE/ASCENT(S)/DESCENT(S) USED

....

....

....

COMMENTS (walking companions, weather, observations, experiences etc)

....

....

....

....

....

....

....

....

....

....

....

....

START LOCATION ....

DATE(S) WALKED ....

START TIME: .... FINISH TIME: ....

ROUTE/ASCENT(S)/DESCENT(S) USED

....

....

....

COMMENTS (walking companions, weather, observations, experiences etc)

....

....

....

....

....

....

The profile of High Spy
looking south

HIGH SPY

Low
Scawdel

CASTLE
CRAG

Borrowdale

If a visitor to Lakeland
has only two or three hours
to spare, poor fellow, yet
desperately wants to reach
a summit and take back an
enduring memory of the
beauty and atmosphere
of the district...............
let him climb Castle Crag.

START LOCATION ....

DATE(S) WALKED ....

START TIME: .... FINISH TIME: ....

ROUTE/ASCENT(S)/DESCENT(S) USED

....

....

....

COMMENTS (walking companions, weather, observations, experiences etc)

....

....

....

....

....

....

....

....

....

....

....

Skye : The Old Man of Storr and his family

START LOCATION ....

DATE(S) WALKED ....

START TIME: .... FINISH TIME: ....

ROUTE/ASCENT(S)/DESCENT(S) USED

....

....

....

COMMENTS (walking companions, weather, observations, experiences etc)

....

....

....

....

....

....

....

....

....

....

....

....

START LOCATION ....

DATE(S) WALKED ....

START TIME: .... FINISH TIME: ....

ROUTE/ASCENT(S)/DESCENT(S) USED

....

....

....

COMMENTS (walking companions, weather, observations, experiences etc)

....

....

....

....

....

....

....

....

....

....

....

....

Dovedale

START LOCATION ....

DATE(S) WALKED ....

START TIME: .... FINISH TIME: ....

ROUTE/ASCENT(S)/DESCENT(S) USED

....

....

....

COMMENTS (walking companions, weather, observations, experiences etc)

....

....

....

....

....

Crag End Beacon

START LOCATION ....

DATE(S) WALKED ....

START TIME: .... FINISH TIME: ....

ROUTE/ASCENT(S)/DESCENT(S) USED

....

....

....

COMMENTS (walking companions, weather, observations, experiences etc)

....

....

....

....

....

....

....

....

....

....

....

....

....

START LOCATION

DATE(S) WALKED

START TIME: _____ FINISH TIME: _____

ROUTE/ASCENT(S)/DESCENT(S) USED

COMMENTS (walking companions, weather, observations, experiences etc)

START LOCATION

DATE(S) WALKED

START TIME: .... FINISH TIME:

ROUTE/ASCENT(S)/DESCENT(S) USED

COMMENTS (walking companions, weather, observations, experiences etc)

This full-length view of Thirlmere is excellent. By a cautious scramble a dramatic aerial prospect of the dam directly below may be obtained, *but extreme care is necessary here: the precipice falls away suddenly and vertically.*

START LOCATION ....

DATE(S) WALKED ....

START TIME: .... FINISH TIME: ....

ROUTE/ASCENT(S)/DESCENT(S) USED

....

....

....

COMMENTS (walking companions, weather, observations, experiences etc)

....

....

....

....

....

....

Entrance to Wark Forest

START LOCATION ....

DATE(S) WALKED ....

START TIME: .... FINISH TIME: ....

ROUTE/ASCENT(S)/DESCENT(S) USED

....

....

....

COMMENTS (walking companions, weather, observations, experiences etc)

....

....

....

....

....

....

....

....

....

....

....

....

START LOCATION ....

DATE(S) WALKED ....

START TIME: .... FINISH TIME: ....

ROUTE/ASCENT(S)/DESCENT(S) USED

....

....

....

COMMENTS (walking companions, weather, observations, experiences etc)

....

....

....

....

....

....

....

....

....

....

....

....

Bassenthwaite, from Ullock Pike

START LOCATION ....

DATE(S) WALKED ....

START TIME: .... FINISH TIME: ....

ROUTE/ASCENT(S)/DESCENT(S) USED

....

....

....

COMMENTS (walking companions, weather, observations, experiences etc)

....

....

....

....

....

....

....

....

....

....

....

....

ASCENT FROM BINSEY LODGE
620 feet of ascent : 1 mile

BINSEY

— 1400 —

heather   heather

heather   — 1300 —

— 1200 —

Start the climb
from a sheep-pen
(two gates) off
the Bewaldeth   Occasional boulders
road. A sketchy   — 1100 —   met on the ascent
track will soon   make comfortable
be picked up, but   bracken   seats for the weary
when it ceases
to gain height   — 1000 —
leave it and
make for   Binsey
the top.   Lodge   → IREBY 2
                          900 —

BEWALDETH 1¾ ←   Binsey Cottage

                                              → ULDALE 1½

Good fellwalkers, like   800 —
good mountaineers,
never walk where   → OVER WATER 1
they can ride.
Bus No. 71 goes   CASTLE INN 2 ←
past the Lodge.

looking   This gentle uphill walk is
west·north·west   quite as easy, but somewhat
                        longer, than appearances
                        suggest. The summit is not
                        in view from Binsey Lodge.

START LOCATION ....

DATE(S) WALKED ....

START TIME: .... FINISH TIME: ....

ROUTE/ASCENT(S)/DESCENT(S) USED

....

....

....

COMMENTS (walking companions, weather, observations, experiences etc)

....

....

....

....

....

....

Honister Crag

....

....

....

....

....

....

START LOCATION ....

DATE(S) WALKED ....

START TIME: .... FINISH TIME: ....

ROUTE/ASCENT(S)/DESCENT(S) USED

....

....

....

COMMENTS (walking companions, weather, observations, experiences etc)

....

....

....

....

....

....

....

....

....

....

....

....

START LOCATION ....

DATE(S) WALKED ....

START TIME: ....   FINISH TIME: ....

ROUTE/ASCENT(S)/DESCENT(S) USED

....

....

....

COMMENTS (walking companions, weather, observations, experiences etc)

....

....

....

....

from Lanefoot

cows
sitting down
(explanatory note)

START LOCATION ....

DATE(S) WALKED ....

START TIME: .... FINISH TIME: ....

ROUTE/ASCENT(S)/DESCENT(S) USED

....

....

....

COMMENTS (walking companions, weather, observations, experiences etc)

....

....

....

....

....

....

....

....

....

....

....

....

START LOCATION ....

DATE(S) WALKED ....

START TIME: .... FINISH TIME: ....

ROUTE/ASCENT(S)/DESCENT(S) USED

....

....

....

COMMENTS (walking companions, weather, observations, experiences etc)

....

....

....

....

....

....

....

....

....

....

....

....

....

Patterdale

115

START LOCATION ....

DATE(S) WALKED ....

START TIME: .... FINISH TIME: ....

ROUTE/ASCENT(S)/DESCENT(S) USED

....

....

....

COMMENTS (walking companions, weather, observations, experiences etc)

....

....

....

....

....

....

....

....

....

....

....

....

START LOCATION

DATE(S) WALKED

START TIME: FINISH TIME:

ROUTE/ASCENT(S)/DESCENT(S) USED

COMMENTS (walking companions, weather, observations, experiences etc)

" .... a lovely peep around a corner...."
(direct ascent from Loweswater)

START LOCATION ....

DATE(S) WALKED ....

START TIME: .... FINISH TIME: ....

ROUTE/ASCENT(S)/DESCENT(S) USED

....

....

....

COMMENTS (walking companions, weather, observations, experiences etc)

....

....

....

....

....

....

....

the Kinniside Stone Circle

looking north-east

Knock Murton   BLAKE FELL   GAVEL FELL   HOPEGILL   GRASMOOR
                                              HEAD

START LOCATION ....

DATE(S) WALKED ....

START TIME: .... FINISH TIME: ....

ROUTE/ASCENT(S)/DESCENT(S) USED

....

....

....

COMMENTS (walking companions, weather, observations, experiences etc)

....

....

....

....

....

....

....

It is a remarkable fact that the Kinniside Stone Circle, although a wellknown ancient monument, is omitted from Ordnance Survey maps. The explanation seems to be that at the time of the first, and early subsequent, surveys, the Kinniside Stone Circle was non-existent, all twelve stones having long before been taken by local farmers for use as gateposts and building materials. But forty years ago a grand job of restoration was accomplished by an enterprising working party, to whom great credit is due. Having cleaned out and measured the sockets in the ground in which the stones were originally set, they searched for — and located — the original twelve, recovered them all, and completely restored the site. Today the circle is exactly as it was when first laid out, thousands of years ago, waiting to surprise the next Ordnance Survey team. *Note for survivors of the working party : one stone is loose.*

START LOCATION ....

DATE(S) WALKED ....

START TIME: .... FINISH TIME: ....

ROUTE/ASCENT(S)/DESCENT(S) USED

....

....

....

COMMENTS (walking companions, weather, observations, experiences etc)

....

....

....

....

....

from Scalehill Bridge

START LOCATION

DATE(S) WALKED

START TIME: FINISH TIME:

ROUTE/ASCENT(S)/DESCENT(S) USED

COMMENTS (walking companions, weather, observations, experiences etc)

START LOCATION ....

DATE(S) WALKED ....

START TIME: .... FINISH TIME: ....

ROUTE/ASCENT(S)/DESCENT(S) USED

....

....

....

COMMENTS (walking companions, weather, observations, experiences etc)

....

....

....

....

....

....

....

....

....

....

....

....

START LOCATION ....

DATE(S) WALKED ....

START TIME: .... FINISH TIME: ....

ROUTE/ASCENT(S)/DESCENT(S) USED

....

....

....

COMMENTS (walking companions, weather, observations, experiences etc)

....

....

....

....

....

....

....

CARROCK
FELL

START LOCATION

DATE(S) WALKED

START TIME: FINISH TIME:

ROUTE/ASCENT(S)/DESCENT(S) USED

COMMENTS (walking companions, weather, observations, experiences etc)

START LOCATION ....

DATE(S) WALKED ....

START TIME: .... FINISH TIME: ....

ROUTE/ASCENT(S)/DESCENT(S) USED

....

....

....

COMMENTS (walking companions, weather, observations, experiences etc)

....

....

....

....

....

....

....

....

....

....

....

GOOD PLACES TO STOP, REST, EAT AND DRINK

NAME/LOCATION   COMMENTS

NAME/LOCATION   COMMENTS

GOOD PLACES TO STOP, REST, EAT AND DRINK

NAME/LOCATION   COMMENTS

....

....

....

....

....

....

....

....

....

....

....

....

....

....

....

....

....

NAME/LOCATION COMMENTS

GOOD PLACES TO STOP, REST, EAT AND DRINK

NAME/LOCATION	COMMENTS

NAME/LOCATION	COMMENTS

The Lunch House

GOOD PLACES TO STOP, REST, EAT AND DRINK

NAME/LOCATION   COMMENTS

NAME/LOCATION	CHARGE	COMMENTS

GOOD PLACES TO STAY OVERNIGHT

NAME/LOCATION	CHARGE	COMMENTS

NAME/LOCATION	CHARGE	COMMENTS

Wasdale Head

GOOD PLACES TO STAY OVERNIGHT

NAME/LOCATION	CHARGE	COMMENTS

NAME/LOCATION   CHARGE   COMMENTS

Some Personal notes

Douglas fir

Douglas Fir

Scots pine

Scots Pine

143

Roe buck

Baby
roe deer

Sitka spruce

Sitka Spruce

Larch

Japanese Larch

winter

summer

PICTURE LOCATIONS AND CREDITS

The illustrations used throughout come
from the following books by
A. Wainwright:

Pictorial Guides to the Lakeland Fells
Book 1: The Eastern Fells
Book 2: The Far Eastern Fells
Book 3: The Central Fells
Book 4: The Southern Fells
Book 5: The Northern Fells
Book 6: The North Western Fells
Book 7: The Western Fells
The Outlying Fells of Lakeland
The Pennine Way Companion
Westmorland Heritage
A North Wales Sketchbook
A Second Lakeland Sketchbook
*Scottish Mountain Drawings, The Western
Highlands*
Scottish Mountain Drawings, The Islands

[Publisher's Note: Where possible the
location shown in the illustration is
included but where no title or location
was mentioned in the original book the
source alone is quoted.]

Front cover: (*Book 5*)
Endpapers, front and back: (*The Pennine
Way Companion*)
Title page: (*The Pennine Way Companion*)
p. 2–3 Stob Bàn 3274′, Achriabhach
(*Scottish Mountain Drawings, The Western
Highlands*)
p. 4 (*Book 7*)
p. 5 (*Book 5*)
p. 6 (*Book 6*)
p. 8–9 (*The Pennine Way Companion*)
p. 10 The Ravenglass and Eskdale Railway,
Irton Road (*The Outlying Fells of
Lakeland*)
p.11 (*The Pennine Way Companion*)
p.12 (*The Outlying Fells of Lakeland*)
p.13 (*The Pennine Way Companion*)
p.14–15 The top of Deep Gill, Scafell (*A
Second Lakeland Sketchbook*)

p.16 (*The Outlying Fells of Lakeland*)
p.17 (*Book 4*)
p.18–19 The mountain skyline seen from
Beinn Bharrain (*Scottish Mountain
Drawings, The Islands*)
p.20 The Hanging Stone, Base Brown
(*Book 7*)
p.21 19th-century monument, Muncaster
Fell (*The Outlying Fells of Lakeland*)
p.23 Circular sheepfold, Wiley Gill, Great
Calva (*Book 5*)
p.24 Blencathra from Clough Head (*Book 1*)
p.27 Malham Cove, Yorkshire (*The Pennine
Way Companion*)
p.29 Rock formations on Green Pikes
(*The Outlying Fells of Lakeland*)
p.30 Broad Stand, Scafell (*Book 4*)
p.31 (*The Outlying Fells of Lakeland*)
p.32 The Island of Rum, from the
mainland (*Scottish Mountrain Drawings,
The Islands*)
p.34 Signpost, Kirkstile Inn road junction,
Mellbreak (*Book 7*)
p.36 (*The Outlying Fells of Lakeland*)
p.37 Limestone pinnacle, Penyghent
(*The Pennine Way Companion*)
p.39 Ullswater from the north-east ridge
of St. Sunday Crag (*Book 1*)
p.40 Brae Fell from the Caldbeck road,
near Fell Side (*Book 5*)
p.42 Moss Eccles Tarn, Claife Heights
(*The Outlying Fells of Lakeland*)
p.43 Wise Een Tarn, Claife Heights
(*The Outlying Fells of Lakeland*)
p.44 The Pudding Stone, Coniston Old
Man (*Book 4*)
p.46 Swindale with Selside Pike at the
head of the valley (*Book 2*)
p.47 Swindale Head (*Book 2*)
p.48 Path in the heather. Caldew Valley at
the base of Knott (Carrock Fell in the
background) (*Book 5*)
p.51 View from Gatherstone Head,
Yewbarrow (*Book 7*)
p.52 Gray Bull, The Wet Sleddale

THAT
BLOODY
WAINWRIGHT!